Eliana Briel

Different Notions of 'Culture'

GRIN Publishing

Bibliographic information published by the German National Library:

The German National Library lists this publication in the National Bibliography;
detailed bibliographic data are available on the Internet at http://dnb.dnb.de .

Imprint:

Copyright © 2012 GRIN Verlag GmbH
Print and binding: Books on Demand GmbH, Norderstedt Germany
ISBN: 978-3-656-88177-3

This book at GRIN:

http://www.grin.com/en/e-book/287928/different-notions-of-culture

GRIN - Your knowledge has value

Since its foundation in 1998, GRIN has specialized in publishing academic texts by students, college teachers and other academics as e-book and printed book. The website www.grin.com is an ideal platform for presenting term papers, final papers, scientific essays, dissertations and specialist books.

Visit us on the internet:

http://www.grin.com/

http://www.facebook.com/grincom

http://www.twitter.com/grin_com

Different Notions of 'Culture'

For all this apparent ubiquity, the term 'cultural studies' remains an unusually 'polysemic' sign. (Millner/Browitt 1)

The academic field of 'Cultural Studies' has experienced a major worldwide growth in the last 25 years of the 20th century. (cf. Millner/Browitt 1) Everyone uses and discusses the abstract noun 'culture', but its exact meaning varies to such an extent, that it seems necessary to examine the different notions of culture: As a matter of fact, 'culture' is one of the most complex words of the English language; only 'nature' denotes more meanings. (cf. Eagleton 1) One can say that there is hardly anything that is not culture.

To begin with, the consultation of a renowned dictionary provides a first glimpse of the polysemic use of 'culture'. According to the *Collins Cobuild Advanced Learner's English Dictionary* the term signifies the following (342):

1. *Culture* consists of activities such as the arts and philosophy, which are considered to be important for the development of civilization and of people's mind. [...]
2. A *culture* is a particular society or civilization, especially considered in relation to its beliefs, way of life, or art. [...]
3. The *culture* of a particular organization or group consists of the habits of the people in it and the way they generally behave. [...]

In order to further investigate the different notions of 'culture', it seems necessary to approach the concept historically. The field of Cultural Studies arose from the postwar debate about the nature of social and cultural change. (cf. Hall 12/22) New developments such as mass media, mass society and England's role in a postcolonial world, were taken into account. In 1964, Richard Hoggart founded the Centre for Contemporary Cultural Studies (CCCS) in Birmingham, in order to engage in the matter of cultural change as "politics by other means." (Hall 12) Thus, the field of cultural studies as a multidisciplinary approach to culture, with literary criticism as its main constituent was born. (cf. Milner/Browitt 6)

According to Stuart Hall, Hoggart's deputy and later successor, the field had developed out of the *Crisis of the Humanities* whose followers expanded the current meaning of elite-culture to popular culture. (cf. Assmann 220f) Furthermore, they were concerned to treat culture as warplace of identity politics, to rearrange their literary canon and to demand an increased inclusion of social and cultural minorities. (cf. Assmann 30). Pioneering works were Hoggart's *Uses of Literary* (1957) and William's *Culture and Society 1780-1950* (1958). (cf. Hall II., 13f) Their main aim was to engage in 'real' problems, to bring together practice and theory, as well as to figure out how the world works. (cf. Hall 17f)

1

Raymond Williams' *Culture and Society 1780-1950* attached four meanings to culture: "an individual habit of mind; the state of intellectual development of a whole society; the arts; and the whole way of life of a group or people." (Milner/Browitt 2) Apparently, he dismissed the first meaning "an individual habit of mind." (Milner/Browitt 2), but later on reintroduced it, grouped the second and third meaning together and contrasted them to the fourth "anthropological" meaning (cf. Milner/Browitt 2f). In a later work, Williams differentiated between three definitions of culture: the 'ideal', the 'documentary' and the 'social' one. (cf. Williams 48) The 'ideal' would be culture as "a state or human perfection, in terms of certain absolute or universal values." (Williams 48) Secondly, the 'documentary' critically analyses culture as "the body of intellectual and imaginative work, in which [...] human thought and experience are variously recorded." (Williams 48) Thirdly, the 'social' definition describes "a particular way of life." (Williams 48) Cultural tradition at last is a sum of continual (re-)selection and interpretation, "a part of man's general evolution, to which many individuals and groups contribute." (Williams 56) Thus, it is an active process. Williams claims that those three general categories must be equally included in any adequate theory of culture. (cf. Williams 50) His approach to the concept of 'culture' demonstrates the complexity of its idea:

> [It] is nowhere more graphically demonstrated than in the fact that its most eminent theorist in post-war Britain, Raymond Williams, defines it at various times to mean a standard of perfection, a habit of mind, the arts, general intellectual development, a whole way of life, a signifying system, a structure of feeling, the interrelation of elements in a way of life, and everything from economic production and the family to political institutions. (Eagleton 36)

The Yale professor of English and Comparative Literature, Geoffrey Hartmann also differs between the general idea of 'culture' and one specific culture (cf. Milner/Browitt 4) Furthermore, he suggests culture as a counter position to society and as one of the four fields to which politics, society and economics also belong (cf. Milner/Browitt 4): "While for Williams society still remained a generality, or a commonality, for Hartman it has already become a multicultural plurality of particulars." (Milner/Browitt 4) Andrew Milner and Jeff Browitt argue that 'culture' can be seen as a concept of civil society, as introduced by Marx and Weber, which forms together with politics of the state and economics of the market a trichotomy. (cf. Milner/Browitt 5)

One of the most complete definitions of 'culture' is provided by Aleida Assmann in her *Einführung in die Kulturwissenschaft*: She differentiates between six uses of the term of which the first three are value-free and the latter ones value-bearing (cf. 13/17):

Firstly used in the second half of the 17th century, the term 'culture' derives of the latin root *colere* and originally referred to an activity: the "tending of natural growth, either in animals or in plants" (Milner/Browitt 3) This legacy can still be seen in the terms 'agriculture' and 'horticulture'. (cf. Assmann 13) Assmann's first use of 'culture' refers, hence, to any human occupation that is systematically pursued, cared for, cultivated and upgraded. (cf. 13) Andrew Edgar and Peter Sedgwick argue similarly that 'culture' starts "at the point at which humans surpass whatever is simply given in their natural inheritance" (102) or as Terry Eagleton puts it: "culture is just everything which is not genetically transmissible." (34)

Assman's second use refers to geographical and political formations such as different nations and their unique developments. (cf. 13) Whatever keeps a nation or specific group united, be it its own language, mentality, values, customs or way of life, can be summarized as its respective culture, examples are the English or the Eastern culture. (cf. Assmann 13) Edgar and Sedgwick point out, that cultures often live on, "even though the individuals who built them die." (103) Moreover, Assmann's third use is inclusive, ethnographical and universal, in the sense that it describes everything that constitutes the living together of human beings: all fields of human life and experience can be culturally examined. (cf. 13f)

Fourthly, from the 19th to the middle of the 20th century, the bourgeoisie laid claim on a normative definition of 'culture' which was engaged in 'high' or elite culture. (cf. Assmann 14f) By studying canonical texts, they set themselves apart from the lower classes. Assmann's fifth use is another normative terminology of culture, connected with civilization. A nation can be called civilized or cultured, when its citizens control their natural instincts and constantly practise self-discipline. (cf. Assmann 15f) At last, 'culture' can refer to a critical counter world that opposes reality. The 'Frankfurter Schule' has distrusted all cultural goods categorically; it opposes for example the triumphs of popular mass culture. (cf. Assmann 16f)

Taking all notions of culture into account, one has to admit that the abstract term cannot be summarized under one heading. The Collins Dictionary, Raymond Williams, Geoffrey Hartmann and Aleida Assmann agree that one notion of 'culture' refers to a particular society and its unique way of life. Moreover, 'culture' seems to treat human activities which might strive to human perfection, define an elite culture or are connected to whatever is being done and being internalised. Obviously, narrower and broader senses of culture are omnipresent, question the usefulness of 'culture, but also demonstrate its importance.

Works Cited:

Aleida **Assman**, *Einführung in die Kulturwissenschaft: Grundbegriffe, Themen, Fragestellungen* (2006; Berlin: Erich Schmidt, 2006), esp. 11-30

Terry **Eagleton**, *The idea of culture*, 1. publ.., (Oxford: Blackwell, 2000)

Andrew **Edgar** and Peter **Sedgwick** (eds.), *Key Concepts in Cultural Theory* (London: Routledge, 1999)

Andrew **Milner** and Jeff **Browitt**, *Contemporary Cultural Theory: An Introduction*, 3rd ed. (1991; London: Routledge, 2002), 1-10, 128-133

Stuart **Hall**, "The Emergence of Cultural Studies and the Crisis of the Humanities" (1990), in: *October, Art, Theory, Criticism, Politics*, Vol. 53 (MIT Press, Summer 1990): 11-23

Stuart **Hall** II., "Die zwei Paradigmen der Cultural Studies", *Widerspenstige Kulturen*, ed. Karl H. Hörning/Rainer Winter (Frankfurt: Suhrkamp Taschenbuch Wissenschaft, 1999): 13-17

Collins Cobuild Advanced Learner's English Dictionary, 5th ed. (Glasgow: Harper Collins Publishers, 2006): 342

Raymond **Williams**, "The Analysis of Culture" (1961), *Cultural Theory and Popular Culture: A Reader*, ed. John Storey, second ed. (1994; Harlow: Pearson, 1998): 48-57